Texas Estate Planning Myths
and Other Tall Tales

Debbie Cunningham

Table of Contents

Introduction

I am a planner by nature. Nothing makes me feel better than a goal, a plan to get there, and a list that I can check off along the way; so, it is no great surprise to those that know me that I ended up in estate planning. Estate planning allows me to work with individuals, couples and families to ensure their loved ones are protected and their wishes are honored. But some planning is more difficult to think about and sometimes to implement.

As we all know, life does not always go according to plan. One day our lives will end. Some will be blessed with good health, a long life and a quick end that does not involve illness. Unfortunately, at least one of these three things will elude most us. To manage these unknowns, you need to have an estate plan in place. Estate plans are not only for the wealthy; they are for anyone who has loved ones, property or investments. Your estate plan should be tailored to your unique needs. It can be as simple as beneficiary statements and powers of attorney or as complicated as tax planned wills, trusts and more.

Even if we know we need to plan for the unexpected, it is not any fun to think about. As a result, having a Will and Powers of Attorney prepared is on the to-do list, but then never gets checked off. After all, it requires making an appointment with a lawyer, possibly taking off work, spending some money and finally thinking about all the unpleasant things that might happen to you.

Here is your opportunity to find out why estate planning should be a priority. Each of these myths tells real life stories about how having a plan saved the day, or how the lack of one brought hardship and grief.

Myth #1: I am too young for a Will.

NOT TRUE!

There is a belief that only old people near death should have a will. If we all lived to be old, or we all knew when we would die, then waiting until you were old or near death would be an appropriate time to have your Will prepared. Since people die at all stages of life and often without warning, no one is too young for a will.

When it goes right....

A few years ago, I helped a couple who was "too young" for a will, and it made all the difference. George and Mary were both in their twenties and had three children, one from Mary's prior relationship, whom George was in the process of adopting. They had traditional wills that left everything to each other and equally to the kids.

Within six months of preparing these documents, George was diagnosed with cancer. He fought the disease for nearly three years, but ultimately lost the battle. His willingness to see that he was not "too young" provided great assistance to his widow, Mary. The Will allowed her to quickly get into court and take control of the assets. Winding up his estate was quick and easy.

When it goes wrong...

Henry came to see me after his mother, Lynette, passed away unexpectedly at 43. She had a reaction to some prescription medication which resulted in her loss of life.

Lynette did not have a Will and, like George, was a member of a blended family. She was married and had four children from a previous relationship. Her estate was very small and her heirs needed to collect on one small claim. This would have been quite simple with a Will.

Instead, without the existence of a will, it was necessary to file a Determination of Heirship. This allows the court to identify the heirs but is more costly and time consuming than a traditional probate. Ultimately Henry was able to collect the claim and distribute it among the heirs, but if Lynette had a Will, it would have been quicker, simpler and less expensive.

The client's perspective...

Planning for the future can sometimes feel morbid but Debbie made the situation much more comfortable. She was never demanding and always took the time to explain which documents we needed and why they were important to our plan. Debbie exceeded our expectations and made the estate planning process a positive experience.

I always take the time to refer Debbie to people who need help with their plans. I tell them, "She is the perfect person to help get your documents in order."

- Bill Bates

Myth #2: I don't own anything, so I don't need a Will.

NOT NECESSARILY TRUE!

If you have children, then you have a reason for a Will. Your Will determines who will raise your children if they are minors when you pass away. Additionally, if you pass as the result of an accident, your estate could be the owner of a lawsuit and the resulting proceeds.

If you don't have a Will that designates who should care for your children, then a judge may be making that decision for you. If the child's other parent is still living this may not be an issue. However, if there is no surviving parent, then the courts are required to consider individuals in the order designated in the statutes. This may not be a person you would want to care for your child. Additionally, if people of equal standing all file for custody then the children can be dragged through the court system.

Consider the Johnson children whose parents went out

for dinner and lost their lives in a traffic accident. The Johnsons did not have Wills. Both sets of grandparents were very involved in the lives of their grandchildren and both filed for custody. All of the grandparents were likely acting out of love for the children. However, the children spent the next year in and out of the court system answering questions about all of the grandparents while grieving the loss of their parents.

Today's modern families can make this process even less clear. If all of the children do not have the same parents, then all of the children do not have the same options. While you can never prevent a natural parent from gaining custody, you can designate a guardian for the children if there is no parent. This can reduce the disruption to the family by keeping as many of the children together as possible.

Unexpected deaths cause problems beyond guardians for your children. Sally discovered this when she lost her adult son Tyson in a car accident. Sally was no longer married to Tyson's father, and Tyson had not seen his father in over a decade. Tyson was a young man and didn't have a Will. If Tyson had had a Will, his probate would have been simple and straightforward. The executor would have been appointed quickly and been vested with the legal authority to pursue that claim. Not only that, but Tyson would have designated who received his assets.

Tyson's accident left his estate with a potential lawsuit that could bring a considerable settlement. Without a Will, there had to be an heirship proceeding to establish his heirs and appoint an administrator. Since Tyson wasn't married and had no children, his parents were his heirs. Any heir can initiate the heirship proceeding, but all heirs must receive notice of the proceeding. Sally initiated the proceeding but the estrangement between Tyson and his father made both locating and notifying him of Tyson's death difficult.

Once Tyson's father was located, he could have filed a competing application to be appointed as the administrator for his son's estate but did not. He inherited one half of his son's estate in the absence of a Will dictating otherwise. I suspect Tyson might not have wanted his estranged father to benefit in this way.

This situation could have been even more tangled if Tyson had had a child. In that case the child, not Tyson's parents, would have inherited but, if the child were a minor, someone else would be the administrator of the estate. This creates two different problems. First, who will administer Tyson's estate, and second, who will manage the assets the child receives.

The child's mother could petition to be the administrator of the estate, but Tyson's parents may be able to as well if Tyson was not married to the mother of his child. A judge would then determine who is most suitable for the appointment. Should that be the mother of the child? Should that be Tyson's father, who has not been in the picture? Should it be Tyson's mother? Who has values most consistent with Tyson's? Who is the most qualified? It is not possible to predict whether a judge would use the same criteria as Tyson to appoint this administrator.

Once the administrator is selected and Tyson's estate is ready for distribution to his child, the second problem raises its head. Most people think the mother already has the right to receive these assets for the benefit of her child, but often that is no true. What happens next is a guardianship proceeding for the child, creation of a trust under the direction of the court or assets are deposited into the registry of the court. All three of these options require some court action to initiate and ongoing court action to make the funds available for the child's benefit. If Tyson had a Will, he would be able to designate who should manage the assets and how they should be managed with no court oversight.

A scenario that is even less clear arises if Tyson was living with someone or was engaged. That person may have no rights at all. Once again, do you think that would be Tyson's wishes? While it may difficult to think about and may seem very expensive to young adults, estate planning allows one's wishes to be made known, no matter how old one is!

Myth #3: I don't need a Will because everyone knows what I want.

MAYBE!

Everyone may know what you want, but that doesn't mean they will do it. Additionally, the law may not allow them to do what you want or it may require them to jump through many hoops to accomplish your wishes.

If there isn't a Will, the state statutes direct distribution of the estate. The statutes also dictate who has standing to file for probate. In some situations, this is adequate to deal with all of any issues that may arise. What if the facts are not neat and clean? What if the family is not in contact or doesn't get along?

Like Sally in Myth #2, an accident claimed the life of Janice's newly engaged adult son, Robert. Robert had lived with Phyllis, his fiancée, for several years. His father, Bob, had been out of the picture for years.

Phyllis had no legal standing for probate or for receiving any of the property from the estate. Over the years Phyllis and Robert had purchased many home furnishings together. They had a shared account that was used for joint expenses such as rent and groceries. He had purchased a car for her, but there was still a loan which was in his name only.

Since she and Robert purchased items together, Phyllis had to prove the items were co-owned to assert her right to receive some of the assets based on the total value of her contribution to the shared assets. She had no rights to the car because it was titled in Robert's name, the loan was in his name, and car payments were made from his personal funds. There was no documentation proving he gave the car to her.

Because Phyllis had no legal standing to apply for probate or to receive any assets from Robert's estate, she was a legal outsider to the proceeding. Anything she received or consideration given was a gift from Janice and Bob. Janice and Bob each inherited one half of Robert's estate and had equal standing to apply for probate. Although Janice applied for probate and was appointed administrator, Bob had to receive notice of the proceeding even though he had been estranged from the family for some time. It is unlikely Robert would have wanted his father to inherit anything, but at this point, it was too late.

Phyllis was fortunate. She had a good relationship with Janice, and Bob immediately stated an intent to surrender any assets to which he was entitled. Janice knew her son loved Phyllis and had begun building every aspect of his life with her. She took steps to recognize and honor that relationship. The result was that Phyllis was able to keep their joint furnishings without having to prove her ownership interest. Phyllis took over the car payments, and once the loan was paid, Janice transferred the title to her. Although Janice took some family heirlooms from her son's estate, the bulk of Robert's estate was transferred to Phyllis.

If Janice had not had a good relationship with Phyllis, or if Robert had been estranged from both parents, this story might have ended very differently.

The loss of a child is never easy for the parents who have to bury them. However, the pain of this loss can be compounded if the adult child does not have a Will. A Will provides direction to those left behind for how all of the loose ends should be tied up.

The client's perspective...

When my husband passed away suddenly, I was in a state of shock and completely overwhelmed. He didn't have a Will or any other estate plan documents in place, and I knew it was going to be a mess. My husband had children from a prior marriage, and when they got involved in the arrangements, I didn't know how we were going to work it all out.

A friend referred me to Debbie Cunningham because she is very experienced with Probate when there isn't a Will in place. Upon meeting her, I knew she was the right person to help me. She was very calm and she made me feel like my case was a priority for her. I had just lost my husband, and I needed someone to listen to me. What kept me sane was knowing that Debbie was taking care of the legal issues, and I didn't have to be worried about it.

She was on top of everything, especially with the short time frame, and pressured others to keep things moving forward at all times. Debbie is conscientious, diligent

and very hard working. She makes things happen!

*Debbie made sure I got the fairest possible outcome –
it was such a relief. She walked me through it every step
of the way, and I leaned on her for everything- social
security issues, veteran's benefits and even closing on the
sale of my house.*

*If you have someone that passes away without a Will,
especially with stepchildren or a blended family, I would
highly recommend Debbie Cunningham. It can be very
complicated but Debbie really knows what she's doing.*

–E.O.

Myth #4: I don't need a lawyer to prepare my Will. I can do it myself.

MAYBE!

Many of us embrace the do it yourself (DIY) lifestyle. Why pay someone to do something you are fully capable of doing yourself? In some cases this is wise money management, but it can also be a disaster in the making.

Consider the plight of Jane's children. Jane received a medical diagnosis that ensured her death many years before expected. She left behind four children (4, 8, 12, and 15 years), a life insurance policy and a modest estate. She desperately wanted to protect her children, so she bought a book and prepared her Will.

The book allowed her to create a legal Will with the proper witnesses and execution formalities. She appointed her sister as the executor and left her estate and life insurance policy to be equally distributed to her four children. The book didn't explain or she didn't understand that children under 18 couldn't own or manage property; so the life insurance proceeds which normally pay directly to the beneficiary were subject to a guardianship proceeding.

A court-appointed guardian of the estate would be required to manage the funds left to the children, and the associated fees would reduce the money available for their care. This would also delay availability of the funds for the care of the children. If Jane's Will had created a testamentary trust for the care of her children, the life insurance would have been paid immediately to the trustee and would be available for their care.

Jane also neglected to appoint a guardian for her children. The father of the older three had been out of the picture for several years. The youngest was the result of a brief affair, and her father was only an occasional visitor in her life. Because the biological fathers have first priority in a custody consideration, these siblings could have been separated, since Jane's will didn't state otherwise.

The court gave Jane's sister temporary custody of the children while the fathers were located and directed that the life insurance proceeds be deposited into court-created trusts for the children. Jane's sister was made Trustee of the trusts as well. Over the next year, the children found themselves talking with judges, social workers and the fathers they did not know well.

Ultimately the children were adopted as a group by a close family friend while the sister continued acting as Trustee of the trusts. This solution was created and agreed to by all parties but it required a great deal of time, effort and money. Is this the solution Jane would have wanted? If so, she could have accomplished it by designating these friends as guardian in her Will, and her children would have been spared the court proceedings.

Each of us leaves a unique signature on the world when we pass. Your Will should be tailored to the needs of the situation you will leave behind. You may prefer the DIY method, but this should be done with extreme caution. If the Will does not dispose of all of your property, have appropriate language for an independent administration, or include a self-proving affidavit to name a few problems, you could actually increase the cost of probating your estate.

The client's perspective...

I was attending one of Debbie's presentations about the importance of creating an Estate Plan when it dawned on me that I had not updated my Will after my marriage. I have three young children, one from a previous relationship, in a blended family and it's important that they are protected if anything should happen to me.

Until I met Debbie, my future planning documents consisted of a "Will in a box" I had purchased long before getting married and having a family. Those types of Wills work for single individuals who don't have any large possessions, but I no longer fit into that category. My wife and I realized it was time to hire a professional to help us map out our future.

Debbie made me realize the importance of creating a custom estate plan by describing situations that never crossed my mind. No family is a cookie-cutter case, and their estate plan shouldn't be either. Her ability to communicate complicated issues and put them into perspective made the process much more pleasant.

Debbie takes a positive approach and knows how to

address the sensitive topics. She is very professional but still relates to people and their concerns for the future. I would recommend Debbie to anyone who wants to work with a down-to-earth, family-focused attorney.

–Fred Campos

Myth #5: I have a Will from another state, so I am covered.

MAYBE!

It is true that all states recognize Wills prepared in other states. However all Wills are based entirely on state law, so you should have any out-of-state Will reviewed by an attorney. The Will may be effective in Texas but not provide for an independent administration, have a self-proving affidavit or fail to conform with the Texas requisites of a Will. These features make the probate process in Texas quicker and easier. Furthermore, if you are moving from a non-community property state your Will may not address what is to be done with the community property you have acquired in Texas. In that case, the community property will pass according to the state laws of descent. This may create the desired result but in todays complicated family structures there may be an unintended gift to a family member not of your choosing.

You will also want to find out how Texas treats your assets and family members. In some states, all property goes to the spouse in the absence of a Will or with partial intestacy. In Texas, property will only go to the spouse if all of the children have the same two parents. In today's blended families, that can result in an unexpected and potentially undesirable distribution.

While an out-of-state Will is often better than no Will, it comes with its own set of potential problems. An up-to-date Will in your state of residence will always serve you better.

Myth # 6: I don't need a Will because we all get along.

MAYBE!

However, that does not always hold true in the grief that can follow a death.

Betty and Anthony had been happily married for 15 years when he became ill. She stood by him as the illness progressed and eventually claimed his life. They did not have any children together, but Anthony had a son and daughter from his first marriage. Betty and her step-children were friendly but not close.

Anthony died without a Will. He and Betty had lived a modest life, and he felt there was not enough there to worry about. However, that is not the way things turned out. Anthony's children wanted all the family heirlooms and anything else the law might entitle them to receive. They hired a lawyer and demanded Betty turn over their inheritance.

The Texas statutes addressing inheritance state that if

the children of the person who has died are not all also the children of the surviving spouse, then the community property does not go to the surviving spouse. The surviving spouse retains their own half of the community property but the community property of the person who died is divided among that person's children. In this case, Anthony's children each got half of his community property, or one fourth of Anthony and Betty's community property.

The difficulty often arises in how to divide the assets. The children are entitled to one half of the value of the assets, but they cannot prevent Betty from remaining in the house or force her to sell the house. In your typical case you create an inventory of the assets and assess a value. This value is then divided in half to determine how much the surviving spouse can retain and what goes to the children.

In Anthony and Betty's case, they owned a home, 2 cars, household furnishings, they each had an IRA and a modest checking and savings account. Betty sold one of the cars and gave the kids the family heirlooms. Each child also owned 1/4th of the home. If Betty decided to sell the home, the children would collect according to their ownership share at the time of the sale. Otherwise they will collect when Betty dies and her estate is distributed.

If Anthony had a will he could have prevented this family discord. He could have given his share of the community property to whomever he chose. This would at the very least have prevented the legal battle.

The client's perspective...

Debbie handled my best friend's Last Will and Testament prior to her passing. She and her husband had recommended Debbie to me after the sudden unexpected passing of my Dad. I interviewed several other attorneys over the phone that seemed to be monetarily focused. I chose Debbie to represent my Dad's Estate due to her extreme compassion during an emotionally stressful time.

Although a written Will was not created prior to his passing, he did express his wishes to many other family members. Unfortunately, his widow did not concur.

Debbie explained the Texas probate process and each step involved in disputing an estate without a Will. She constantly side noted difficult legal verbiage to layman terms, ensuring the understanding of my responsibilities. She was the perfect mediator for this extremely tense and sensitive situation.

I always felt like I was her #1 client. She was even gracious enough to travel two hours away to attend hearings. Her remarkable service was at extremely fair rates. She met and exceeded all my goals and expectations – 10 out of 10!

I continue to HIGHLY recommend her to all those in need of Probate, Wills, and Estate Planning.

- J. G.

Myth #7: It has my name on it, so it's mine.

MAYBE!

Texas is a community property state. If you are married, there is a presumption the property is community and you must prove it is not.

Community property is property acquired by either spouse during marriage with two exceptions. First, property received by gift, devise or descent is separate property. Devise or descent is property received from the estate of a person who has passed away. Second, during marriage, any recovery for personal injuries by a spouse is separate property unless the recovery is for loss of earning capacity during marriage.

Separate property is also property acquired before marriage. However, if you comingle separate and community property, the separate property may lose its separate property characterization. This can happen when you deposit separate property money into a community property bank account.

For example, if you and your spouse buy a house after you are married, it is community property. However, if one spouse purchased the home before the marriage and then the other spouse moved in after the marriage, the house is the separate property of the purchasing spouse.

Although there is a presumption that all property owned by a married person is community property, this presumption can be challenged and, with proper evidence, be classified as separate property.

For example, you buy a vehicle while you are married, but only your name shows on the title and loan. There is still a presumption it is community property owned by both spouses. Even though Texas is not a "name on the title" state, if you can prove the vehicle was purchased with separate property assets then it is separate property.

What about property acquired in another state? It is important to note in Texas the answer is different in a divorce and probate proceedings. In a divorce proceeding, the property will be characterized as "quasi community property" and treated as the other community property. In a probate proceeding, the property will be characterized according to the laws of the state where it is located.

Myth #8: Everyone / No one needs a Trust.

FALSE!

In estate planning, there are no absolutes. The plan needs to be tailored to the needs of the individual and their assets, which means some estates need Trusts and others do not.

Texas is both a probate friendly and property ownership friendly state, which means Trusts are not the necessity they may be in other states. However, if you own investment property in the state, you should consider moving it into a Trust or business entity to provide liability protection. This will also facilitate property management and transfer during incapacity and after the owner has passed.

While Texas is probate and property ownership friendly, it can only control what is within the state borders. If an estate holds property outside of the state, there will have to be an ancillary probate in that state. So if you own property outside of the state, you may want to own it in Trust. This will allow the property to transfer immediately to the intended beneficiary upon your passing and bypass all probate proceedings.

Trusts can also be helpful for certain beneficiaries. Minors cannot own or manage assets. A testamentary Trust in your Will can ensure the assets are available for the care of the minor and are under the control of your preferred Trustee. Additionally, a special needs beneficiary may need to receive their inheritance in trust to avoid disqualification from needs-based benefits.

These are some of the more common reasons for a Trust. However, Trusts are often used for charitable gift giving, planning for blended families, caring for pets, educational gifts and many other purposes.

Myth #9:
Trusts are the only way to avoid probate.

FALSE!

Trusts that are properly funded can avoid probate, but other strategies exist. Financial accounts, life insurance and retirement accounts will pass outside of probate based on the beneficiary statements or payable on death (POD) statements. Regular review of these designations can allow significant assets to pass outside of probate.

Texas, as well as some other states, has a Transfer on Death Deed which works much like a beneficiary statement. A properly prepared, signed and filed deed will allow you to transfer Texas real estate property outside of probate.

Additionally, the Texas Department of Motor Vehicles (DMV) has two options for passing vehicles outside of probate. While living, you can prepare and file a survivorship title. This will transfer your car, boat or trailer to the designated person upon your passing. In cases where there is only a traditional title, no Will and no other assets requiring a court supervised Heirship, you can use an Affidavit of Heirship form provided by the DMV.

Not only that but a Trust with a non-compliant Trustee can land you in probate court anyway. Just as in Myths 3 and 6, things don't always go according to plan. A Trust created for probate avoidance is only as good as the funding, the Trustee you appoint and the clarity of the Trust language.

If you fail to transfer any assets into the Trust, then there may be a need for probate to address transfer of those assets into the Trust or directly to the intended recipient. A fully funded Trust with a Trustee who is refusing to follow the terms of the Trust may require the Trust beneficiaries to take action in probate court against the Trustee. In other cases, Trust language that is ambiguous can result in a dispute with the probate court determining what that language means.

Trusts can be great planning tools. They can solve many problems, address many issues and allow you to provide for different family groups in a blended family. Unfortunately they are not a silver bullet and may lead the beneficiaries into probate court anyway.

The client's perspective...

I wanted an experienced attorney who recognizes the sensitive nature of a case involving family members. My children's great-grandfather passed and left them as beneficiaries to a trust. The trustee was supposed to transfer the trust over to my wife via a special directive but had not done so. I needed an attorney who understood the complexities of trust law and the probate system to represent my children's interests.

Debbie was very in tune with our needs. She understood that my family's relationships were strained, and I wanted to avoid further tension. Debbie understood my family values and never let me lose sight of the bigger picture. Preserving family relationships was just as important as fulfilling the special directives.

She really took the time to understand the personalities involved in our case and had the perfect balance of sensitivity and forcefulness that I was seeking. Her measured approach kept us out of court and resolved the matter, which is what we were looking for.

Debbie's strategy and timing was impeccable from start to finish. She provided personalized and exceptional service. I'm convinced that if it wasn't for Debbie, we'd still be battling it out. Without a doubt, I would recommend Debbie to anyone needing representation.

- A.F.

Myth #10: If I am incapacitated, my family can take care of everything.

MAYBE!

Your family may be willing to take care of everything, but what does everything entail and do they have the legal right to do that?

A family member with a key can bring in the mail, check the house for security purposes and care for a pet. However, they will not be able to pay your bills, sell property or make any financial decisions on your behalf. A Power of Attorney will be required for someone to manage your financial decisions for you.

A Power of Attorney (POA) allows you to designate the person of your choosing, along with one or more alternates, to manage your affairs. Your POA can give very broad authority, allowing your agents to do anything for you that you could do yourself, or it can give more limited power to address only the issues you find most critical.

The POA deals strictly with financial issues. If someone needs to make medical decisions for you, then a Medical Power of Attorney will be required (MPOA). Once again you can designate the person of your choosing along with one or more alternates to step into your shoes for these decisions. An MPOA can never be used to overrule your decisions. It is effective only when you cannot make a decision.

In addition to naming your preferred decision makers, both the POA and MPOA allow you to exclude individuals that should not have authority. Additionally, you do not have to name the same people in both documents. The person best suited to paying your bills may not be the person best suited to make medical decisions. These documents do not prevent your family from discussing the issues and working together, but they do allow you to determine who is making the decision if there is a disagreement.

The client's perspective...

Debbie is a golden resource and she really knows estate planning. She is direct, informative and always ready to help. Debbie truly is a hidden treasure.

-B. Fenson

Conclusion

I hope you found this book helpful and learned something new. Perhaps it answered your questions or maybe generated some new questions you didn't know you needed to ask.

It is my goal to help people understand how the law treats them and their loved ones during the difficult times that accompany incapacity, disability and loss of a loved one. We can work together to put in place the pieces of an estate plan that will ensure loved ones are protected and your wishes are expressed and followed.

You may have seen your story in these pages or may have seen a similar situation play out in the life of another. If so, and you are looking for someone to help ensure your story is the "worked out right" version, I would be happy to assist you.

You can find more information on my website www.irving-law.com. Appointments can be made by calling 972.426.2835 or emailing apptepm@irving-law.com.